MOM

The Woman Who Made Oatmeal Stick to My Ribs

JAMES MICHAEL PRATT

SHADOW
MOUNTAIN

*"All that I am, or ever hope to be, I owe
to my angel Mother"*

—ABRAHAM LINCOLN

Library of Congress Cataloging-in-Publication Data

Pratt, James Michael.
   Mom, the woman who made oatmeal stick to my ribs / James Michael Pratt.
      p.   cm.
   ISBN 1-59038-253-6 (Hardbound : alk. paper)
   1. Mother and child—Miscellanea.   2. Parent and adult child—Miscellanea.   3. Gratitude—Miscellanea.   4. Conduct of life—Miscellanea.   5. Mothers—United States—Biography.
   6. Pratt, James Michael—Family.   I. Title.
   HQ755.85 .P733 2004
   306.874'3—dc22   2003023985

Printed in the United States of America   18961-014P
R.R. Donnelley and Sons, Crawfordsville, IN

10   9   8   7   6   5   4   3   2   1

Contents

Contents

From *Dad, the Man Who Lied to Save the Planet*

CHAPTER 1

Appreciation for
Everyday Moms

*"Youth fades, love drops, the leaves of friendship fall; a
mother's secret hope outlives them all."*

—OLIVER WENDELL HOLMES

I figure my mom was pretty much typical of
mothers of her generation. The daughter of a
mother who had been born in the late 1800s, Mom
had inherited a set of values and moral teachings
that were almost universally accepted in America
in the years when my parents were raising me and
my siblings.

Mom did her best to instill in her children, who
were born in the 1940s, '50s, and '60s, those virtues
that she was confident would bring us success and

1

happiness and ensure we would be honest, decent citizens.

Mom had seven sons and two daughters. Later in life, she also adopted an adult—my third sister. In her selfless devotion to our family, Mom lived the values she was trying to instill in her children.

Like millions of moms her age, Mom grew up in the milieu of the Great Depression of the 1930s, waited for her soldier boyfriend to come home from World War Two, the world's greatest military conflict of all time, and denied herself comforts unknown to previous generations in favor of her children having the best she could provide.

That selflessness is the chief characteristic of mothers, and it is one of the reasons why our mothers occupy such a lofty place in our memories. "Mom" is the sacred and affectionate title we reserve for the woman who gave us life, the woman who we know best, the woman who always put our needs above her own. That selflessness alone qualifies moms for sainthood.

The memories described in this book not only illustrate my mother's virtues but also recognize the goodness of all mothers. I am sure my memories are typical of the stories you could tell about the ways your mother blessed and shaped your character through her teachings and example.

But my mom is, after all, the only mom I have had direct experience with. Remembering and writing down these things has been fun and given me an even greater appreciation for my mother and the direction she pointed me in life. My hope is that my experiences with her will be of interest to you and cause you to reflect with gratitude on your unique relationship with your own mother.

If by chance you did not have a positive experience and missed growing up under the protective wings of an angel mother, I offer you mine, hoping you might find in her example the inspiration to more fully appreciate your own mother. If you are a mother, perhaps you'll discover something in my mom's approach to childrearing that will inspire and encourage you in your own selfless work to shape and mold your children's characters.

Mom, we can never say "thank you" enough. These words pay tribute to you and all the everyday mothers who build the world, one soul at a time!

CHAPTER 2

The Woman Who Made Oatmeal Stick to My Ribs

"Sometimes the strength of motherhood is greater than natural laws."

—BARBARA KINGSOLVER, NOVELIST

Wholesome goodness is what moms are all about. What mom hasn't gotten up before her children to make sure they were nourished and ready for the world?

"I'm late. I don't have time to eat," we say.

"You can't go to school without something in your stomach," our moms counter.

And so we take a hurried moment to bolt down what she has prepared.

Behind the rib cage, close to that stomach that

each morning anticipates breaking the nightly fast, is the heart. All moms know that the heart needs nourishment too. In fact, until the stomach is filled, the heart cannot patiently endure Mom's loving counsel. So mothers wisely feed first and teach second.

I grew up under the wings of a woman whose outlook had been shaped by conditions she had lived through in the Great Depression. Economic hard times had been both a cruel and a thorough schoolmaster, and Mom's attitude toward education, health, morals, and provident living was the product of real and often harsh experience. There are many such lessons of life and values I learned from her, which I now recall as I watch her slip into old age, a new age of mothering, as shocking a realization to me as it is to her. But she is still here and still giving guidance — still reminding me to eat correctly, be safe, and say my prayers.

"M'm, m'm, good!" That famous jingle originating in 1931 still rings in my ears after all these years. In fact, if life on earth were snuffed out, and travelers from a distant planet arrived seeking to understand how we had lived and what caused our demise, they might draw a conclusion or two from what they would find in America's pantries.

There they would doubtless discover several cans of Campbell's Soup, a brand that could be called "America's Official Soup" because it is so ubiquitous. The other item most likely to be discovered would be round, cardboard canisters of oatmeal.

An alien arriving from deep outer space, landing on an earth devoid of living human beings, might radio these initial findings back to his superiors on the mother ship:

"It would seem that the American humans subsisted mainly on two foods. One of them is a liquid mixed with a variety of plant and animal parts. The other is a dry, dusty meal that one can only assume would be hard to swallow. In fact, if eaten in the quantities it appears to have been consumed, it might well be one of the chief killers of this civilization."

"Explain your conclusion."

"The dusty meal appears to be almost inedible, due to its dry nature. One would almost certainly choke and die from asphyxiation, unless the meal were mixed with some form of liquid, perhaps the soupy liquid found in the cans."

"And you say this dry meal is to be found in almost every dwelling?"

"Yes, Commander. And it appears to come from a single, central source."

"Explain."

"Each of the containers of this flat, grainy substance displays the likeness of a round-faced, rosy cheeked, white-haired, and cheerful-looking male, wearing a black cloak and a broad brimmed head covering of some type. A *hat*, I believe the former inhabitants called it."

"And this *hat* would signify leadership of the American tribe?"

"It appears so. No doubt they respected him greatly, for his image is always found on these containers of what they called 'Quaker Oats.'"

"We shall call it *oatmeal*, for the record," the commander responds. "Is there any way of knowing what may have induced the inhabitants to consume this dry meal in such large amounts?"

"Perhaps. In one habitation, we found a written

message next to the carton containing the dry food."

"A communication?" the commander in the mother ship responds excitedly. "It might contain valuable, even secret information — perhaps from the happy male himself — their leader," he adds.

"Yes, Commander. Or might I suggest this message comes from the feminine side of the race. Everywhere, we find images of these American females preparing foodstuffs."

"Then a message from a female American to the happy man you described?"

"That may be so. Shall I send the message to you through our portable translation screen?"

"Proceed."

"Scanning." The alien on the ground passes the note through the handheld device, beaming it up to the command ship.

The words pop up on the screen before the alien commander, seated at the control console of the command ship. He reads:

"Jimmy. Don't forget to eat your oatmeal. It will stick to your ribs. Love, Mom."

In illustrating a truth, sometimes it is useful to

take something to the absurd. Mom was not sophisticated, but she had the knack of unconsciously using metaphors to communicate her teachings. The oatmeal speech she frequently gave us is one such example. In her desire to fortify us against the day ahead, Mom would often say, just as the imaginary mother above, "Eat your oatmeal, children. It will stick to your ribs."

My younger brother, Rex, the brother I grew up closest to—you know, the one you blame for the mischief you get into, cheat at board games, take advantage of and ask to test the cold water of the swimming pool first—was in the hospital a few years back, awaiting major surgery that would take the surgeon through his rib cage.

I had promised that our family would pray for him, and I called him to let him know I was aware of his needs the hour before the surgery was to take place. He was in a well-known Los Angeles hospital, and I had expected merely to leave a message for him. Somewhat sedated from the effects of prep drugs, my brother personally picked up the phone in his private room. Our conversation went something like this:

"So, Rex, you worried?"

"No . . . not . . . really . . ."

"I'm praying for you."

"Oh . . . well, uh, I'm . . . kinda . . . drug . . . ged . . . right now."

"Well, I know everything will go well."

"Oh . . . O . . . kay . . ." he slurred as the drugs took greater effect. "I'd . . . bet . . . ter . . . go . . . now," he added, drifting away from the conversation.

"Can you do something for me?" I asked.

"What?" he demanded, but as kindly as he could under the circumstances.

"Ask the doctors a question when you come out of recovery."

"What?"

"Ask them if they found any oatmeal."

"What?" he squeaked out. "I got . . . ta . . . go . . . 'Bye . . ."

"'Bye. Love you, Brother."

Click.

The surgery was a success, and when I called Rex the next day to check on him, I just assumed he would remember our preoperation conversation of the day before.

"So," I said. "The prayers worked."

"Yeah. Guess so," he answered.

"You ask the doctors the question?"

"What question?"

"You know. They cut through your ribs to get to that gland and fix it, right?"

"Yeah . . . so?"

"So did they find what I asked you to have them look for?"

"Jim, what are you talking about?"

"Oatmeal. Did they find any oatmeal stuck to your ribs?"

Silence.

Rex was still under the influence of the drugs he had been given and wasn't yet thinking clearly, so I let him off the hook.

"Talk to you later," I said. "We are remembering you in our prayers. But ask the doctors for me, will you?"

"Yeah . . . sure. 'Bye."

Click.

See, Mom never lied. Unlike our Dad, who lied

to get into World Ward II so he could save the planet, Mom always told the truth. I'm not sure if she ever mentioned it to any of her other children, but Mom definitely had always told me when I lived at home: "Jimmy, eat your oatmeal, it'll stick to your ribs . . ."

Today my own kitchen cabinets are full of oatmeal—all flavors. I still eat the stuff regularly. But I never quite understood what Mom meant by it "sticking to my ribs." I have never asked either; I just assumed if she said it would stick, then it would.

I recall as a boy feeling around my ribcage after eating my oatmeal and wondering if it took a trip other foods didn't. Maybe oatmeal really did hang out down there.

" . . . and it'll keep you warm," Mom would add, an assurance that eating the entire bowl would be good for me.

See, I trust Mom. So I had never in my life, not even to this day, in my fifth decade, asked why she thought oatmeal, above all other foods, would adhere to my ribs instead of becoming digested in the normal way.

The idea that I took from Mom, especially when I was living thousands of miles away from home in South America, and eating almost daily a soupy gruel of watered-down, cooked oats for breakfast (consumed as a drink rather than a thick porridge) was that oatmeal was good for me and that it would also somehow keep me safe. It was a comforting thing. Whenever I brought the cup of warm, soupy oat drink to my lips, Mom was there with me.

As I think on it now, the oatmeal must have comforted Mom too. She just needed to know that something she did would stick to us away from home, when we seven boys and two girls ventured out into the cold, hard world.

Oatmeal might not literally stick to ribs, but I never, ever, eat it without hearing Mom's voice. So it wasn't just the oatmeal that stuck to this boy. The porridge was a symbol of something else that would stay with me—her love and pride in me and the time-tested values she taught, which provided real warmth and a shield against the punches life would deliver. Obeying Mom by eating the hot cereal was a way of assuring myself that I could succeed.

Mom always got it right, because she always gave the best. There are no perfect moms or dads, any more than there are perfect children; but some moms come pretty close. After all is said and done, knowing Mom cares makes a boy feel safe.

And as for the oatmeal, every time I eat it I smile and think about it sticking to my ribs in a special way, a way that causes me to silently say:

"Thanks, Mom. Your warmth and caring has stuck where it matters most, and it still is protecting my heart!"

CHAPTER 3

"Do unto Others As You Would Have Them Do unto You"

"I think it must somewhere be written, that the virtues of mothers shall be visited upon their children."
—CHARLES DICKENS

The Golden Rule is perhaps the most commonly known and widely accepted standard for personal behavior that exists on the planet. This notion of treating others as you would like to be treated is the foundation of every moral and law-abiding civilization known. Imagine the wonderful effect it would have in the world if everyone lived by that simple maxim. Ours would be a civilization devoid of war, crime, famine, and even many diseases, along with a host of other social ills.

It might sound simplistic, and it might seem a cliché, but the best policy is and always has been to consider how you would like to be treated before dealing with another.

Mom tried to instill that mentality in her sons. Based on her own experience, she knew that we boys would likely grow up to witness war and even face devastating hunger, illness, and various privations. She also knew that *The Golden Rule* would be one of the best medicines for the negative circumstances we would encounter.

All of us are faced daily with situations that don't seem quite right or even fair. Life offers no guarantee of evenhanded treatment. Moms worry about this, and rightly so. In the event a bully would show up or an opportunity to cheat, fib, or slip into dark and forbidden paths would come our way, Mom knew that being morally prepared would be the best answer to the challenge.

It was spring, 1965, and I was late for school.

"Remember, Jimmy, do unto . . ." she called as I raced out the door and started my run to Knolls Elementary School. " . . . others . . . " I heard halfway down the block.

"Yeah, sure, Mom," I mumbled as I waved her off. "Whatever . . ." I answered under my breath.

Why does she always have to say that? As if I don't understand or something? I posed silently as I ran the five blocks up Christine Avenue, to see if I could squeeze into class under the tardy bell.

I liked to run. In fact, I enjoyed most sports. I was always competing and loved the challenge to my sixth-grade body to see if I could run all the way without giving in to walking. I'm pretty sure I made it to school just before the bell rang for starting classes.

It was the early 1960s, and the hills of our somewhat rural town, located just over the northern Los Angeles county line, were beginning to sprout suburban neighborhoods. It was not unusual for a new family with kids to move in every couple of weeks. I always enjoyed learning where the new kid was from and generally making friends.

Meeting these newcomers, I remembered what it was like moving to this new town. Being uprooted from established friends and familiar playgrounds had not been an easy thing for me.

Without going through any mental gyration of

19

why having more friends was better than having fewer, I usually tried to make friends the first day a new boy or girl would show up. I didn't know it at the time, but looking back I can clearly see that Mom's daily admonition had an irresistible effect.

So, when I noticed the new kid, Phil Piraino, I decided to make a friend, to make him feel comfortable. Besides, he might come in handy after school when we chose up teams for games or playing war in the wide-open fields and rocky hills that surrounded our home.

I had another friend at Knolls Elementary who didn't have the same idea about how to greet newcomers. Mark May was a tough kid. I recalled two years earlier when he had first bullied me — given me arm burns, twisted my right arm behind my back, and administered various other minor tortures to see how much I could take. I had made a friend of him more for safety's sake than a desire to have him for a buddy. Mark liked being in charge, and I knew he would probably test my new friend, Phil, his first day at school.

During morning recess, I was standing in the ball line — the line that formed outside the sports equipment room where all kinds of balls could be checked out—footballs, basketballs, those big red bouncy rubber balls that the girls really liked in four-square games, and softballs and bats. By the time I finally got the last basketball, a crowd had gathered near the hoops.

"Hey! Stop it!" I heard Phil complain.

Uh-oh, I thought, stopping dead in my tracks. The crowd grew noisier.

"Punch him, Mark," someone shouted.

"Fight back," another called.

If I just walk away and pretend I didn't see this, if I just let it go and not get involved, I won't end up with a bloody nose or worse.

The problem was that Mom's words kept ringing in my ears: *Jimmy, do unto others . . .*

Yeah, but, Mom, this is not me doing anything wrong, it's Mark May, I protested to the voice inside. " . . . *as you would have them do unto you,*" she finished. "Ohhh . . ." I moaned as I moved forward.

"Hey! Mark!"

"Hey what, Pratt!" he called back as I broke through the crowd. Mark had Phil in the familiar arm lock and was twisting him to the ground. Tears were starting to form in the new boy's eyes.

"Leave him alone!" I said, mustering all the courage I could.

"You gonna make me?"

"Yeah. Maybe I will."

I didn't have a clue how I was going to back that up or why I had even said it. Mark was grinning from ear to ear with a look that said: "Oh, boy! Two people to beat up. This is my lucky day." He still had Phil in the arm lock.

I moved forward again. "Let him go, Mark!"

Mark's face turned from a grin into a puzzled expression.

I moved closer. "I mean it. You're gonna have to fight me too!" I said, as I put up my fists.

I could tell Mark was weighing the consequences. Maybe two scrawny kids could take him on and then he'd lose face with everyone else. If he lost face, then he'd lose power. Or worse, he'd lose face and have to answer to the principal and the long wooden paddle Mark had already become familiar with.

"Oh, go on!" he huffed, letting Phil go. "I'll get

you later, Pratt!" he barked as the bell rang for recess to end.

That day I made a new friend and also reinforced a bond with Mark May that lasts until today. I don't quite understand what it is about Mark that I liked. Maybe it was because once you became his friend he was truly loyal to the core. We had a lot of good clean fun in years to come, and though he was admittedly on the wild side with other types of friends, Mark paid me one of the ultimate compliments a few months after my twenty-first birthday.

I had recently returned home to Simi Valley, California, from South America where I had been doing volunteer work for two years, and had just spoken about my experience to our local church congregation. After the meeting I was standing outside the chapel, greeting well-wishers, when out of the corner of my eye, I saw a familiar and sturdy young man in blue jeans and T-shirt come bursting through the glass doors into the foyer.

"Jim! I heard that you were home!" Mark said as he pushed through the crowd and gave me a big hug.

"Man, it's good to see you! You are the only friend who never let me down. You know that?"

I was stunned. I stammered something like, "Thanks, Mark." Then we caught up on old times. Before he left the building and I went my way in life and he his, he smiled and said, "I still wish you would have let me beat up Phil Piraino." We laughed and had our little secret. Mutual respect had been earned years before. I treated both Mark and Phil how they would have wanted on that spring day in early '65, and Mom was to blame.

I was given a payday that Sunday morning that I have never forgotten. Over the years, I had remained friends with both Phil, the Italian kid whose parents had immigrated to the United States after World War Two, and with Mark, the bully.

Maybe Mom was right after all. Maybe when you treat others the way you'd like them to treat you, life pays you back in kind. Like medicine that moms spoon-feed their kids to keep them well, this simple formula for building relationships was given in doses I could swallow.

My world is a better place because of a simple

prescription Mom reminded me to take, and it has worked from the inside out.

Now, as I consider those days of youth, I understand that one of the finest things Mom ever did after the oatmeal was finished was to remind me:

"Remember, son, do unto others as you would have them do unto you."

CHAPTER 4

Mom's Taxi

"A suburban mother's role is to deliver children obstetrically once, and by car forever after."

—PETER DE VRIES

I was reminded of Mom's taxi not long ago when I learned she was stranded in Idaho, needing to make the three-hour trip south to the University of Utah Medical Center for a scheduled appointment.

One of her adult children always comes through. This time it was my turn, and so I drove north the two hundred miles from my home to pay a respect to her that truly cannot be done too often.

See, Mom drove a number of taxis over the years. Her meter was always on, but the riders were never charged. I think on that now, especially as she sometimes needs someone else to be her taxi driver.

Cub Scouts, school days, dances, jobs, shopping. . . . Imagine having to coordinate the comings and goings of nine children, whose birthdates were scattered between 1945 and 1962. Mom was constantly on the run, chauffeuring us from place to place. Being a taxi-mom probably never entered her mind when, as newlyweds, she and Dad bought their first car after World War II. Our parents hadn't had the luxury of a having a taxi-mom or taxi-dad when they were growing up in the 1920s and '30s, during the Great Depression. In answer to our frequent demands that we be driven here or there, they and others of their generation would always say: "When I was your age I walked, and it never killed me."

How many miles did she drive over the years to cart me and my siblings the many places we needed to be? I'm not sure it can be calculated, but the number must be in the hundreds of thousands when you consider the devotion and willingness she showed to make sure we were everywhere we should have been.

"You kids want to go bad enough, you can walk," I remember my father saying more than once, whenever I complained that Mom couldn't immediately take me somewhere I wanted to go.

Of course we had school buses and took those. And we had bicycles and rode those. But when the bike was down or one of the other kids had it, we were taught that there was nothing wrong with walking.

"I walked to school after I had fed the cows and milked them too. And—"

"I know, Dad, five miles, uphill both ways, and through snow with no shoes on," I would finish.

"How'd you know?" he'd counter with a smirk. "Anyway, try walking. It won't kill you."

So we weren't afraid to walk a mile or more. Unlike suburban kids today, we lived in a time when hitchhikers were still picked up without any thought of possible danger and kids were safe to walk alone or in groups on public roads. I often took the hike from our house on Christine Avenue, up to the train tracks five blocks away, and followed them with my roller skates strung over my shoulder to the skating rink on First Street in Santa Susana. It was only three to four miles away, and I never thought it was a big deal—more of an adventure.

We didn't appreciate it at the time, but when Mom could, she'd break away from a dozen other details of life to take us places: Scout meetings, music lessons, school plays, and a variety of other places we needed to be.

Most kids never give a second thought to the thousands of miles his or her mom drives to get them around town during their growing-up years. In the selfishness and thoughtlessness of youth, we just expect Mom to have car keys, gas money, and time to deliver us wherever we want to be. The child sees only the right they have to the trip. A taxi-mom, on the other hand, usually sees the trip differently, viewing the service as a way to enhance her son or daughter's life in some way, while ensuring her child's safety.

"Isn't a mom *supposed* to do this?" one of my children once asked, while being driven somewhere in air-conditioned comfort.

"Maybe, but it's why she does it that matters," I answered.

Whoosh! Right over his head. That part has no meaning and won't until his children ask the same question.

I clearly recall the make and model of all of Mom's taxis. In 1962, our family's 1950-era Cadillac was an embarrassment to me. I can see it vividly—the weather-worn, blue four-door. Dad loved Cadis. They were a symbol of quality in those days and still conjure up that image in any person over forty. From my dad's point of view, to own a Cadillac, regardless of its age, was to own a fine automobile.

Never mind that ours were always ten years old by the time they came to us—they still carried significant appeal with Dad, so we were forced to ride in the heavy beasts with the distinctive taillight fins. Our 1952 model had the rounded fins, not the space-age look of the Cadis of the sixties that we would finally own in the late '70s. No, this Cadillac looked like a movie prop from the early *Superman* TV shows.

The wealthy mobster of Metropolis would drive

this car after having threatened the destruction of the tallest building in town unless the ransom were paid. Then, just as the evildoer, driven by his body-guards, was making an exit to safety, Superman would stop the speeding 1952 Cadillac with one outstretched hand. The evil man would be brought to justice.

In my nine-year-old mind that was the good part of owning the old '52 four-door. I could tie a towel around my neck, dash out in front of it, and pretend I was bringing it to a screeching halt.

I loved the *Superman* show, but in 1962 it was time to forget the past and jet into something more "hip," more "with it."

The '56 Ford and the '57 Chevy in '67 (cars I'd pay dearly to own now), the crumpled-fender, smoke-belching, depression-era dull gray, beat-up hunk-of-metal covering a motor that may have been a Renault brand . . . these were just a few of Mom's taxis that carried us boys to the really important places of our youth.

Air-conditioning was provided by an open window, and the only safety restraints were the other kids, used as a shield during an emergency stop.

But Mom was more than the driver. She also fixed flats, changed car batteries, replaced drive belts, and even did a valve job on the '57 Chevy so Dad wouldn't have to worry about it. She was, and still is, every boy's dream taxi driver.

Mom can't drive anymore. It's not that she doesn't know how. It's just that life's challenges, brought on by age, have limited her availability. Infirmities have slowed her down and required her to "hitch" a ride rather than provide one. And it makes all of us, her children, happy to bring our taxis to her door.

I took her to her doctor's appointment this week and then back to Idaho. No matter how often I make the trip with her, even though it is a four-hour trip each way, it just doesn't seem to be long enough. I can't repay her time—those awfully embarrassing rides she gave in taxicabs of varying ages and disguises.

She cancelled the meter long ago, and I'll never know for sure how much I owe. I only know this: whatever it is she needs, I cannot do enough to repay her. She had the time for me when I didn't understand what that all meant. Now?

Mom, you have the right to ask, and I have the duty to respond. You can ride in my taxi any time.

CHAPTER 5

"Eat Your Food! There Are Starving Children in Africa!"

*"She was ignorant of life and the world,
but possessed a heart full of love."*

— HANS CHRISTIAN ANDERSEN

Ever wonder how the food you didn't eat might have gotten to the starving kids in Africa?

Or India?

Or China?

Or South America?

Or any other place your Mom implied it might have been used if you hadn't wasted it?

What our mothers employed was a great, guilt-inducing strategy. It was designed to get us to eat everything on our plate and to feel guilty if we didn't.

That compulsion not to waste food was something felt very keenly by mothers who had grown up during hard times, when food was hard to come by and simply could not be wasted. But the way Mom said it always made me feel that if I didn't clean up my plate, I was somehow responsible for the starvation of little children in some unspecified, desolate, famine-plagued foreign land.

In these early years of the twenty-first century, Americans are an increasingly overweight society. Blame for that deplorable condition has been laid at the feet of the fast-food industry. But the responsibility clearly belongs to our well-intentioned mothers. It's *their* fault! The accusing finger can now be correctly pointed where the blame belongs.

At *MOM!*

The day before penning this, I was at my older brother Nick's home in California. I hadn't seen him for a year, since four of us seven sons had taken a trip back to the Midwest to visit some Pratt family heritage sites.

Of the four who took that trip, three of us — Grant, Nick, and myself — had, unlike younger brother Rex, faithfully obeyed Mom when it came to eating. We looked it, too. No food was going to get wasted by any of us and make the trip overseas without us.

But Nick has a new look this year, completely unlike the old! He has lost twenty or so pounds, and the difference in his appearance is startling. He has a new image that is obviously very pleasing to him. He looks better, and he feels better.

One of his motivations to lose weight has been his stated goal to live to be a hundred and to do so with vigor. Extremely active and hard working, Nick figures the weight loss is good for the heart.

He still eats everything on his plate, he informed me. It is just 2,000 to 3,000 fewer calories a day on his plate.

"I started a new diet over a year ago, too," I reminded him. During our trip to historic sites last year, I informed my brothers, when they asked me why
I was leaving food on my plate after each meal, that it was, in fact, a new diet that I would one day proclaim to the world.

This is that day.

And the diet is called: *The Starving Child Anti-Guilt*

Trip Started-by-Mom Diet. I told my brother that I hoped that it would debunk the notion that by slicking up our plates, we were helping malnourished children in every impoverished nation on earth.

My brothers laughed, humored me, and finished their meals.

Actually, I can't totally blame Mom and her generation of non-wasters. Her parents and theirs, for one hundred generations before them, were to blame, as was the experience I had while living in South America.

Back then, I was a young, twenty-year-old American male and constantly hungry. If there are two things I remember from the twenty-two months I lived in Peru, they were being hungry and being tired. I learned from that experience to eat everything on my plate or risk going hungry until I would get another stab at a dinner.

In fact, I recall getting to the point where if I found a dead insect floating in my daily ration of soup, I would just pick it out and go on with the meal. I came to understand what my dad had always said, when referring with a laugh to his four-year experience eating World War II Army chow, occasionally flavored by an unwanted pest: "It was just more protein."

So, Mom wasn't totally to blame for the girth my guilty mind had produced. I had just been conditioned by my growing boy's appetite not to waste food or opportunities to eat.

I had gotten a few pounds heavier than my "ideal weight" over the three decades I had officially been an adult. In fact, gaining just a tad over ten extra pounds for every decade, I had ballooned up in ways that were startlingly evident in the mirror or recent photographs. Oh, I had tried several fad diets over the years and had started a number of aborted exercise programs, but I had not done enough to curtail my gradual weight gain.

Surrendering to the fact that there were simply some foods I liked and had no intention of giving up, I was seated in a diner during a business trip one day years ago, determined to listen to my Mom. The voice in my head kept nagging me:

"Jimmy, finish your food. Remember the starving children in Africa!"

"Yes, Mom," I would answer as I dutifully

shoveled the remaining bites into my mouth, over the protests of my uncomfortable midsection.

I later sat in another diner, on the Missouri River near St. Louis, explaining to my three smiling brothers my epiphany. I told them of the moment I finally rebelled against Mom and her vision of feeding the world.

It was somewhere in the South, in some hotel restaurant. I was cramming fritters or chicken-in-gravy-somethings into my mouth, knowing that I shouldn't disappoint my mom. It was as if she were standing over me, observing me eat, compelling me to clean off my plate. But I had reached the point where I didn't think I could take another bite, and I was struggling to finish the down-home portion I had been served.

I was in my mid-forties at the time and still thoroughly obedient to Mom's voice from my youth. There was no way on earth I would let her down or go back on the resolve I had made during my years in Peru—that if I ever got back to the United States I would never waste a plate of food again.

So I sucked it up (literally), sighed heavily, and angled my fork for the remaining piles on my plate.

See, these Southern folks really know how to feed you, and of course, the waitress would check every few minutes (she was probably a mom too) and ask, "Is everything okay?" or, "Is the food all right?"

I couldn't let her down, could I? I mean, what message does it send not to finish food cooked to order? It could hurt her feelings, and I didn't want to do that.

But I had finally had enough. In spite of Mom's nagging, my stomach protested the final few bites. I had a vision of how disgusting I looked and felt with the full face and girth I was wearing around town.

I was telling this story to my three grinning brothers, as we sat in that fabulous Missouri River restaurant just outside St. Louis, with my half-eaten plate of food in front of me.

"Mom lied," I told them.

"Huh?" Grant queried.

"Mom lied to all of us," I repeated.

"Oh, get out of here," Nick barked with a wave of his hand.

"She did," I insisted and looked at Rex who rolled his eyes.

Silence.

"Okay, what did she lie about?" Nick finally asked.

"The starving children," I answered.

"Huh?" Grant asked again.

"Children in Africa don't get what I leave on my plate. She promised all of us, that if we ate all our food the starving children would be benefited. I don't see it that way. If we eat it all how do they get any?"

"Go on," Grant said, ever eager to learn the truth.

Nick just waved me off. Rex grinned.

"See, here I was in this restaurant in Alabama, and I wasn't starving. In fact, I was more than satisfied. But Mom was there looking over my shoulder and reminding me. Making me feel guilty."

"You took Mom with you?" Grant asked.

"He doesn't mean literally," Rex interjected.

"Oh."

Silence.

"Soooo . . . ?" Nick pressed.

"I told her, 'No.'"

"Really?" my oldest brother and namesake of our father asked with incredulity.

"Yes. I told her to go away and leave me alone."

More silence.

"Want to know what I did?" I asked. I love playing the fool for my brothers, though they would tell you I really don't need the practice.

"I told Mom that if I finished all my food, there would, in fact, be none for any children anywhere and that I would never again listen to her or believe her on this issue!"

"What did she say?" Grant asked with a laugh as he turned up his hearing-aid dial a notch.

"She left and has never bothered me again. I think she is mad at me or something."

We all had a good laugh and then enjoyed an hour of small talk about growing up, the nonsense of my logic, and such.

But truly . . . I had rebelled against Mom's premise!

I knew at thirty pounds beyond my normal blood pressure weight that Mom meant well—all moms do. But wasting the food on my plate would not benefit one single child who was going hungry!

It had become clear to me what I should do: rather than worrying about wasting unneeded food, I would simply eat only half of it. And then, someday, I might even consider changing the kinds of food I eat.

I know Mom never meant to lie, just inspire. She was only doing what mothers had promised for generations before her, that by eating everything she had so arduously gathered, managed to pull from the ground, the cow, the goat, or wherever, then prepared, that their children would not starve, that they would be okay. Motivated by motherly instinct and by her love and concern for me, Mom had implied something that wasn't true.

As we wandered back to our hotel, I think Mom was on all of our minds. We were in midlife and full of appreciation for our parents. Many of our children were now entering their own adulthood, and we knew we had certainly perpetuated the same frugality-based motivation Mom told us:

"Eat all your food! There are starving children in Africa."

Well, to the world's shame, there *are* starving children in far too many places. We burn crops and pay farmers not to grow them in the United States so that we can keep prices up.

We could feed the world today—certainly most of it anyway—just from the uneaten portions left on plates like mine as I dine out. I try not to feel guilty about it. I do participate in contributing funds to ease and alleviate the suffering of the poor. I wish my new diet could literally help, that foods wasted were indeed not. I really do.

But it causes me to refocus regularly on the goodness of mothers in their effort to care for, feed, and nourish their children.

Moms everywhere are God's right arm. The compulsion to encourage finishing, not wasting, and eating well, has derived from centuries of knowing that recurring scarcity, droughts, plagues, and economic disasters can and do literally take food off the table.

In her anxiety to nurture and nourish, our mother broke her own rule and told us a lie. We know it now. Nothing we waste on our plates can get to Africa to feed someone else's child.

But Mom's frugality and her determination to never waste, borne of what she had endured in the

Great Depression, are important for us to consider today. We have become a throw-away society, much to the dismay of Mom and mothers everywhere.

We may not be able to transport our uneaten portions overseas to help out other mothers who are filled with anxiety for their starving children's survival, but we can do something about it. We can donate, give, and help those mothers with our surplus wealth. There are charitable organizations we could support by cutting back on half of what we see piled so high on our dinner plates. A dollar a day will go a long way in countries where the head of the house earns less than that.

For now, join me and remember Mom, what she meant, and why she cared so deeply that we learn not to waste.

Why not find a charitable organization that can offer food and clothing to caring but desperate mothers and fathers in other lands?

Mom, thanks for your care. I know there are starving children in the world, and because of you I am doing something about it!

CHAPTER 6

"We're Gonna Eat Who?"

*"My mother had a great deal of trouble with me,
but I think she enjoyed it."*
—MARK TWAIN

My parents, children of a more rural America, were used to eating and canning what their families grew in the garden, raising animals for fresh meat, milking cows and goats, and collecting eggs from the chickens. The few groceries they may have bought from a store merely supplemented their homegrown and home-produced food.

It was not until the 1950s and the growth of the food manufacturing and distribution industries, coupled with new media technologies (such as television) for enhanced advertising, that prepackaged foods became popular in this country. The convenience of prepared foods ultimately turned the family garden in this country into a quaint relic from the past. Nowadays, only in agricultural America are you likely to find a family eating freshly shucked corn or vegetables harvested that morning and using cream skimmed from fresh milk and butter made from that day's dairy production. And the truth is, for the sake of convenience, most contemporary farm families also buy and use prepared foods, rather than go to the trouble of processing something from their garden, orchard, or flock.

For a few of us (those who are older) the freshness of homegrown food and the satisfaction of bringing it directly from the garden to the table is only a distant memory, distorted no doubt by the passage of time. We forget how hard and monotonous the work was and how old-fashioned and embarrassing it seemed for us modern kids to have to do farm work.

For the vast majority of young Americans, that

long-ago practice of producing your own food is now as hard to fathom as it is to imagine living without cell phones or e-mail. Most of today's urban children have no idea that the serving of Chicken McNuggets in their "Happy Meal" was made possible by the recent slaughter of a chicken that otherwise might be clucking and scratching in the dirt of some farmyard.

I constantly badger my wife to be allowed to look for land far from the city, a place to grow our own food, or even grow food to give away. See, growing something takes time, and time invested in something as meaningful as good health and hard work is time well invested.

Circumstances and modern life conspired to prevent me from giving my own children the experience of preparing soil, planting, watering, weeding, and harvesting the results, as well as caring for animals, but my parents, and especially Mom, certainly did not fail to do so for me.

A few years ago, when my son was in his early teens, we were riding together in the car not far from our home, when he pointed to a pasture and said, "That's a funny looking cow."

I was multitasking at the time — trying to drive and manage an open can of soda pop. But the look of amazement on his face made me turn my head to look at what he had spotted. I saw no cows in the pasture as we passed by.

"Where? I don't see any cows."

"There, Dad. Look. Over there!" he said, in an exasperated tone.

I was in the middle of swallowing a gulp of soda pop, and in my amazement, it forced its way back up and sprayed all over my lap. Choking, then half crying from sudden laughter, I pulled to the side of the road and sat there in stunned semi-awareness, trying to comprehend that Mike actually might be serious.

I was finally able to say, "You are kidding me . . . right?"

"About what?"

"You aren't kidding me, then? You really don't know what that is?" I answered, pointing to the animal he had spotted. I now felt a tinge of embarrassment, a feeling that sweeps over a parent occasionally when he knows he has failed his offspring.

"Oh, son! I have let you down! You mean . . . you're sure this isn't a joke?" I looked for any hint of a joke-meister coming back from his face.

Nothing. A blank but somewhat amused stare returned my questioning and hopeful gaze.

"That isn't a cow, Mike," I moaned. I wasn't sure if it was proper to cry now. I just looked up and out my car window into the blue sky and questioned my Maker: *Is there something I really, really need to know about parenting? I didn't mean for things to get this far out of hand. I could use some help now.*

"Yeah, but it has horns, and it's black and white," Mike argued.

"Mama Mia," I finally let slip through a heavily released sigh. "Just because it has horns and is black and white doesn't mean it is a cow! That's a goat!"

That experience with Mike made me wonder if I hadn't shortchanged my own children by not exposing them to some of the lessons I had learned as I was growing up. We were brought up during a time when most people still understood that eggs, though they may come from the store, actually originate with a chicken; that milk isn't produced by the milkman; and that cheese has its beginnings, not in the state of Wisconsin or the homeland of the Swiss people, but in the udder of some animal. My parents, coming from a hardworking stock of rural people, saw to it that my brothers and I participated in producing at least some of the food we ate.

I admit hating it at the time. Doing farm type chores wasn't exactly the cool thing to do during the hip '60s in suburban Southern California. Not even Wally or Beaver from *Leave It to Beaver,* or redheaded Opie from *The Andy Griffith Show,* had to milk cows. Only a few other kids in our neighborhood had anything like farmwork to do. Maybe they were forced to mow the lawn or take out the trash, but feed animals? Milk goats? A few people may have kept some chickens, but it was embarrassing. I wanted my parents to stop with all this farm stuff and just let us be normal, modern people.

But for reasons that seem wise to me now, Mom and Dad gave us a chance to dirty our hands a bit—spading the ground and planting seeds, milking Jezabel, our family cow, along with a number of stubborn milking goats without names, collecting eggs, and feeding and caring for Pancho the steer and the smaller farmyard animals. Our folks made us work everyday.

As I sat in my car pondering my urban son's inability to tell a goat from a cow, a sudden wave of appreciation swept over me—for Dad, but also and especially for Mom, who hadn't allowed us Pratt kids to entirely abandon our agricultural roots or miss the work ethic we learned by doing our chores.

Truthfully, I never liked goats. Still don't. While milking one, just as you would get down to the last squeeze, the stupid thing would deliberately put her hind foot, encrusted with pasture droppings and mud, in the bucket—just to say "thank you" for milking her. As a boy I imagined that was why milk had to be "pasturized," until I was taught in seventh-grade science about French scientist Louie Pasteur who invented the pasteurization process.

But we knew that Mom meant business when she gave out our assigned chores. She was convinced that one of my younger brothers was allergic to cows' milk, and though I wasn't sure that was true I tried not to complain too loudly about having to milk the goats. I had no alternative but to go along, if I wanted my taxi rides around town.

Pancho was one of several steers we raised during my growing-up years. The idea was to fatten him up and then have him slaughtered. It was always a bit hard knowing the animal you fed would feed you one day. I never quite got used to that.

But Pancho, he was a rare one. He came to us already weaned (and spoiled) from the folks who raised him. He was like a big pet and enjoyed "hanging out" with his owners. He would frequently find a way out of his pen and even tried to get into the house through the back door.

Because of his pesky ways — breaking out of his pen, tromping through the gardens, and leaving "cow pies" on the lawns — Pancho often made Mom angry. That was something he shared with us boys — my brothers and I often made Mom angry, too. Kids and steers have a lot in common. They are hard to keep track of, and keep in line, and are constantly on the lookout for something to eat.

We eventually gave up trying to keep Pancho in his pen and ended up moving him from pasture to pasture and finally a few miles to the other side of town to see if he'd quit trying to "hang out" and be human.

See, we all knew his destiny. We didn't want to say it, and we certainly weren't going to let him know, but he was growing fat and ready for the table. I really did not want to see that happen. In fact, as a twelve-year-old boy, I had gotten so used to his antics and personality that I kind of liked the lug. I looked forward to coming home from school and having him mosey to the barbed-wire fence and hang his head over to be scratched.

On one occasion, Mom had taken all she was going to take from Pancho. "Jimmy, get your shoes on and get in the car. We've got to go down to Royal Avenue. Pancho got out and is bothering someone." She got a rope, and we piled into the station wagon.

When we arrived at the place where someone had complained, we found Pancho contentedly munching on their backyard grass. So we roped him and tied him to the bumper. Then Mom taught him a little lesson by putting her foot to the gas pedal.

Pancho bellowed but kept up. He maybe lost a

pound or two but was soon back in his corral. As we were patching the hole he had created in the fence, Mom said, "Pancho, you keep this up and I swear. . . ." She didn't finish the sentence. She didn't have to. I raised my eyebrow and gave Pancho the *You better not mess with Mom if you know what's good for you* look.

It wasn't long afterward, that one of my younger brothers came running up the street toward me as I walked home from school.

"Mom called the butcher! You better hurry if you want to see Pancho!"

Pancho had apparently created some kind of havoc at the hired-out pasture, and Mom had to bring him to the field across from our house. He had seemed to be cooperating lately, and I figured Pancho would just keep being Pancho.

"No!" I remember crying aloud as I took off.

As I ran through the front door, I saw my older brother, Nick, grinning.

"Guess we're having steak tonight," he said.

I hurried out back and across the ditch to the field, and there under a tarp was a hide, a head, and well--Pancho's outline. I was not pleased and decided to have a talk with Mom. But before I could say anything, she said, "Jimmy, do you think Mrs. Piraino would like some beef? Why don't you go ask her?"

I had a word or two with Mom that she couldn't hear and sullenly walked up the street to the Prainos's house. They were Italian and ate parts of a cow I had never before heard of people eating.

I explained the situation to my friend Phil, and his mother came out with the family picnic cooler. "The brains and heart. And tell your mother thank you!" she said with her warm but strong Italian accent.

Well, I was a bit more disturbed than before. I took the cooler home, Mom took care of the rest, and as I carried the cooler back I had a talk with the best parts of Pancho. "You numbskull! I told you not to mess around and be so bull-headed with Mom. Look where it got you!"

My parents taught me a lot about animals, where food comes from, and how to grow our own. I regret my son can't tell a goat from a cow and pray there will always be a grocery store in operation for as long as he lives.

Just as important as learning to work and how to be responsible, were the lessons Mom taught us about respecting life, gratefully using God's creations to sustain ourselves, and accepting the stewardship we had been given over the earth and all it can provide.

As for Pancho, he was hard to swallow. What he should have learned was, *If you know what's good for you, don't say "no" to Mom.* Guess he should have listened like the rest of us. He might have lived longer.

Thanks, Mom, for teaching the values of work and of all God's creations. The lessons you taught me about industry and provident living are with me still.

CHAPTER 7

"Remember to Call Home"

"God could not be everywhere, so He made mothers."
—JEWISH PROVERB

It's been thirty-two years since I permanently left home and first heard Mom call out, "Remember to call home." Over the years I've been obedient to her request and have called home often. I continue to do so, though she lives now in a different house than the one I left as a young adult. But that's okay. Wherever she resides is "home" because she is still *Mom.*

In her later years, Mom has become deaf, so phone calls don't work anymore, but we've found there are other equally good ways to communicate. We now keep in touch through greeting cards, letters, and e-mail. Though her kids are now becoming grandparents, we still receive her prayers, birthday greetings, and frequent messages.

There is a parallel to Mom's reminder that I will share with you. Perhaps as important as anything she taught me is a counterpart to the "call home." It will make more sense as I share some stories with you about her influence across the span of thirty-two years, since I first walked out her door to live on my own.

Mom doesn't know this, but I have kept all her correspondence since my youth. She has always intended to write a personal history and is a gifted writer. But I sense things get in the way. One of those things is the feeling she has that a history of her life couldn't be all that interesting. "Oh, people don't want to read about me. My life hasn't been all that special." So she has been hesitant to sit down and write her history. Fearing she might not ever get to it, I'm building a "Mom's History File" from memories, letters she has written, and now the e-mails we exchange a couple of times each week. Unwittingly embedded in those letters, cards, and notes, are details, facts, memories, and insights that make up the fabric of her life.

Mom, to her amazement and ours, has arrived at an age many call "old," and others kindly refer to as "senior." Aging is a sneaky devil and always a surprise to the protagonist of its tell-tale story. I think Mom is quietly recognizing it is her turn, but even so won't surrender her call to be Mom to her kids and now to her grandchildren and great-grandchildren.

A dozen years or so ago, Mom began doing something her mother always did. When a birthday greeting arrived from our Dutch immigrant Grandma Vorkink, it always came with a crisp one-dollar bill tucked inside. Receiving one of those when we were kids felt like winning the lottery. One dollar could buy a lot of goodies back in 1961.

When I received my first one-dollar-bill birthday greeting from Mom, I was thirty-five. I smiled, felt pleased, and couldn't bring myself to spend it. It still resides in the envelope with that greeting.

It's become Mom's way of sending additional love and a reminder, "Don't forget your mother."

She knows how much we all enjoyed receiving that little token from Grandma Vorkink, but indeed all nine of us love Mom and wouldn't forget her in anyway.

I know the day will come when I will no longer go or "call home" to Mom. But with her words and my memories, that trip will not be necessary. I have the documentation of her life in that file, in the messages she has sent.

Even more important, she will remain with me whenever I need her—in my heart.

Often I consider the memories stored in that center spot beneath my ribs when I spend time corresponding with Mom and on the actual trips I take to Idaho to see her. If there is anything I can do, anything she needs, I'll be there. I know my brothers and sisters feel the same. We all stay in touch, and there is no such thing as *taking turns* to help Mom in her advanced years. She was always there for each of us, and I am proud of my family members for always being there for her now.

For a period of two years, when I was nineteen and twenty years old, I was far from home in the Andean country of Peru. Though I had friends from school and a girl or two I was fond of who occasionally wrote, it was the weekly letters from Mom that kept me going and were the first to be read.

There was always the welcome news from home, of course, keeping me in touch with everything that had ever mattered in my life. But more than that, there was a reassurance that Mom had been thinking about me, that she was still concerned, that she had been praying for me.

There were occasional weeks without mail, but I knew that it wasn't because Mom hadn't written. I had watched her faithfully write to both of my brothers while they were stationed in Vietnam, and I knew I would not be forgotten. Any delay was the fault of the unpredictable Peruvian Postal Service.

During one especially lonesome time, I was living in the Andean valley town of Cajamarca, the city where Pizarro had conquered the Incan King Atahualpa and his force of twenty thousand warriors; being there was a history lover's dream come true. Though the natives were friendly, I was feeling especially far away from home. I looked forward to the weekly letters from Mom.

During December, a particularly rainy month, the mail had been delayed. I'd had no mail for a couple of weeks, and had of course missed getting the news from home. But what I was missing most was the comforting, handwritten message from my mother, which always began, "Dear Jim . . ." and ended with, "All our love, Mom and Dad."

On a particular Monday, my American companions and I stood outside, near the airport, at the precise time the flight was scheduled to arrive with the mail, listening for the familiar sight and sound of the prop-driven, World War II era aircraft.

Home — there is no place like it on earth, even though you become accustomed to another place, and even enjoy it and the people.

Four young Americans, longing for news from the States, yearning for word from Mom and Dad, friends, and girlfriends, eagerly watched for the clouds to break, which would allow the plane to land on the small, mountain valley airstrip bordered by cow pastures and dairy farms. Taking off and landing was tricky business, and the crew needed to be careful. If visibility was limited, they couldn't risk an approach. I didn't blame the pilots for the care they took, especially since I had been a passenger on one of their flights and knew how harrowing the landing could be.

"Come on. Come on," I encouraged. "You can make it. Come on down," I urged the pilot through airwaves he couldn't tune in to. Our countenances dropped and hope flew away as the plane's engines could be heard disappearing, headed back for the clear coasts of northern Peru's city of Chiclayo.

"Maybe Wednesday," I suggested.

"Yeah, if the weather breaks," one moaned.

Wednesday came, then Friday, without success. Then finally, on the following Monday, the plane arrived with packages, mail, and word from family and friends. We were like little kids at Christmas. You'd think we had been starved for days for something to eat. We consumed the news, each letter, over and over. I saved them all and still have them to this day.

One from that week in December 1972 reminds me to write. After the news of the week and good wishes, she penned, "Don't forget to write home. With all our love, Mom, Dad and kids."

Dad's been gone ten years now. But whenever I

get a handwritten letter from Mom, she still signs, "Love, Mom & Dad." We all know Moms do most all the writing anyway, but the gesture is so sweet, allowing Dad to still be part of every communication.

In his later years, Dad was the one we could actually talk to when we called home to check in and give our love to both, but he never was much the writer. Mom, unable to hear, always comforted those of us far from home in the written way, then patiently waited for our replies.

Her teachings, and those of Grandma Vorkink, are etched indelibly in my memory. For as far back as I can remember, both of them used to say each night, "Jimmy, don't forget to say your prayers." That was their way of reminding me to "call home."

Our family, on both sides, had for generations been religious people. Mom's side is full of Dutch immigrant folks who came to America in pursuit of the great dual dreams of freedom and opportunity at the turn of the twentieth century. My dad's people, the Pratts, landed in America a bit after the *Mayflower*, in the early 1600s, and were a part of the New England Pilgrim heritage.

In my parents' home, prayer was as much a formal family rite as was going to church on Sundays. Mom and Dad routinely called us together for what we called "family prayer." Each evening, before retiring, our parents would gather all of us around their bed or in the living room, and one of us would be called upon to say a prayer out loud. As a boy, I didn't question the practice or think of our family as particularly religious. Praying was just one of the things we did together. I just assumed all families did the same.

It was impossible as a child to appreciate the benefits of praying together as a family or what the simple nightly ritual would come to mean to me — especially when the call to prayer often interrupted such favorite television programs as *Bonanza, The Lone Ranger,* or *Combat,* starring Vic Morrow. But now, looking back, I see the wisdom in things and am grateful for the practice and the closeness it promoted in our family. I consider this simple family ritual, as it was observed by my parents, the single most important teaching from home ever bequeathed to me.

It didn't seem possible when I was a child, when

my parents were such pillars in my life, that the time would come when they would become feeble and eventually slip the bounds of this mortal existence. Death visits all of us, although a child seldom considers it possible to lose Mom or Dad. They knew it, though. They knew that there would come a time when they would no longer be around to talk to or lean on. In times of loneliness, doubt, fear, confusion, or even sickness and near death, each of us kids would need another lifeline to cling to—one that would never fail us. I didn't recognize it at the time, but Mom and Dad used that nightly demonstration of faith to instill in each of us another way to reach "home"—from any place on the globe, at any hour, and in the midst of any peril. I was being taught I could always *call home.*

My Grandma Vorkink also did her part to help me learn that lesson.

"Jimmy, I vant to tell you something. Come," she'd say with a wave of her hand.

This would get my attention. Grandma always had a stash of Hershey's chocolate bars with her. She and chocolate went hand-in-hand in my mind, and though some might call it a bribe, it mattered little to me. All I had to do was listen for a few minutes and then she'd break off some chocolate. I'd have to give her a kiss, which I didn't mind either; I loved my Dutch grandmother.

"Jimmy. Alvays say your prayers." And then she would add, "And be vorthy."

"Okay, Grandma." Then I'd get the chocolate and hit the road.

The idea that I needed to talk to God finally registered. Ignoring the urgings of my parents, my Sunday School teacher, and Grandma Vorkink, I had been flopping into bed without talking to God, and in my child's mind, I was feeling pretty guilty.

The year must have been 1960 or thereabouts. I couldn't have been more than six or seven years old, but I can still vividly see the house, the bedroom I shared with five brothers and sisters, and the bed I knelt next to that night as I said my first meaningful prayer. It was the beginning of a nighttime ritual that I have observed ever since.

I do not intend this recitation to be preachy, just an affirmation of a wonderful benefit I gained from having a good Mom and a good grandmother.

Last week Mom and I were exchanging e-mails.

I had been detailing some trouble I had experienced, "calling home," see . . .

"I still pray for you, Son," she wrote back.

My vision got a bit blurry. From over two hundred miles away at her computer terminal, she couldn't notice the catch in my throat.

"Jim, you know what I mean when I say I'm praying for you, don't you?"

"Yes, Mom. I think I do," I typed back.

"You, everyone, individually." She then went on to tell me what that meant in terms of the time she was spending on her knees beside the same poster bed we had all knelt around as children. It was impressive, and I was caught in a moment of immense appreciation for having her for my mother, and in the certainty that God heard her kinds of motherly prayers. I was, in a word, *grateful* to be her son and to know she was still praying for me and my adult needs.

A mother's prayer is a precious thing. Her teaching a son to pray has untold ramifications, I suppose. I teach my children, and the wave of good thoughts and blessings spreads from our lips to God's ears to someone else's home. I can say, without a doubt, that it was Mom, and Dad too, who started it all.

In a larger sense than merely "remember to call home," which we were requested to do by an anxious mother, I was taught that we have that ability as long as we have life and breath, and I learned of the resulting peace and assurance it brings.

Growing older, Mom had earlier questioned what her mission might be at age eighty-one. She asked me: "Why, with husband gone, so many family members, friends gone too, and feeling so useless most of the time, why am I still here?"

"To pray for us, and to let us serve you," I answered. "And, Mom, as long as you are around, we can still call home."

She prays for my health and success as she did when I was a child. Imagine how I feel. Do you really think I don't want the benefit that comes from the connection this tireless prayerful one has with God?

Praying for the soldier sons, now soldier grandsons, extended relations, friends—this is the kind of *old lady* the presidents of nations, kings, leaders of churches, and people in peril need on their side.

Home, not the structure, but the place where the child learns to trust the nurturing parent, is the place Mom chose to teach us to *call home.* Well, churches teach men to pray and so do books, but moms do it best.

Remembering to call home, write home, or e-mail home is one of the finest acts of love we can do for aging parents during our busy routines. I do believe God smiles upon us as we remember the woman who bore us and taught us to talk to Him.

Thanks, Mom, for not only teaching me to pray but for giving me the faith it takes to find the power to do it. Because of you, I know I can always call home.

CHAPTER 8

"Be Still and Be at Peace, Son"

"When you are a mother, you are never really alone in your thoughts. . . . A mother always has to think twice, once for herself and once for her child."

—SOPHIA LOREN, ACTRESS

There is an inner ear that hears something the noisy world cannot offer. Mom taught me this lesson long ago, though even now I am only beginning to understand the magnitude of it all.

Not long ago, I was visiting Mom in Idaho. My sister Karen, who lives next door to Mom's small retirement home, was there with me. Mom had something on her mind.

"Open your mouth so I can tell you are listening

to me!" she barked. We were sitting in Karen's living room, and I was doing my best to show my respect during a rather lengthy explanation of something, and Mom was a little perturbed.

"How can I know you are listening if your mouth is shut?" she scolded. "Now open, be still, and listen!"

I had been watching this same movie for thirty-five years, ever since Mom first lost her hearing in 1967 after corrective surgery to repair her loss of hearing went awry.

But this holding my mouth open so I could hear better? It had me baffled. *Is she merely funning me or is this a new technique?* I thought. Perhaps she had given up on me hearing through my ears so she was insisting I supplement the use of them by offering my mouth as a new hearing aid. Maybe she figured if I opened one more area in the region of my head I was more likely to get what she was saying.

Sitting there with my mouth wide open, I tried not to laugh, and Karen did her best to be respectful. Mom went on for a while, then finally said, "Oh, for heaven sakes, Jim! Shut that mouth of yours! You look like such a fool with it hanging open like that!"

So I shut it and allowed her to go on. Understand, this is my mother, and Mom is an eighty-something, talking to her fifty-something son. See, I still obey. Mom may not still be able to con me with that eat-all-your-food stuff and starving children routine any longer, but if she needs me to listen, I figure it's her right to direct my mouth, ears, or whatever, so that the communication gets accomplished.

I think Mom deserves to be heard when she speaks because she has endured something that would have turned everyone else I know into a cynical, angry soul. Frustrated in the face of an accelerated loss of hearing, in 1967 she opted to have an operation she was led to believe might help. To her surprise and utter despair, she ended up undergoing and paying for an operation that not only didn't help but instead resulted in a 98 percent loss of hearing.

She came out of surgery hoping the ringing in her ears was only temporary. She hoped that she would gradually get back her hearing at least to a level where she was before the surgery. She prayed for a miracle. Her operation was, after all, motivated by her desire to be a better mother, friend, and spouse.

But things didn't improve, and disappointment and frustration grew as the silent years went by. Finally, though, Mom turned a strong will into action. She read about sign language. She read about God, and how to cultivate a positive attitude. She learned to read lips. She never gave up hoping she would regain her hearing and bought a succession of increasingly sophisticated hearing aids. But none of them helped much. We all had to yell, speak clearly, remember to look in her direction, and make sure she was making eye-contact in order to be understood and not have to repeat what we had said.

Many friends and associates, growing impatient at having to repeat themselves, began to shun Mom. It took everything I could do one day to keep from verbally striking back when I watched a woman turn her back on my mother and heard her mutter something unkind about Mom's hearing loss. Such snubs happened more often than Mom could ever know.

Her disability put a strain on many of her former relationships, causing her to depend on only a few understanding and dear friends — people with kind hearts, patient women, like Barbara Anderson. Barbara knew instinctively that listening healed others, and she was always there for her friend Virginia. She is still there today, and the service she has given means the world to us now.

Mom also had a doctor she could talk to, and she developed wonderful and expressive letter-writing skills. Dad was always patient and kind and was never offended, no matter how many times she might have to ask him to repeat himself.

But over time, because of hurt feelings and other's tendencies to dismiss her from their conversations, Mom withdrew inside herself, to a place only she and One other could be. That place was where she found God.

It was precisely at this time of Mom's midlife that she began to reassess everything she had been taught about faith, God, and philosophies for successful living. Reading was an escape to a place she could hear and be heard. And prayer, the kind she taught me, was a private affair that could be done a dozen times a day if she wanted. Maybe others couldn't hear her, but she reasoned, *If God is indeed all He is claimed by writers to be, then He will hear me.*

This is not to say Mom only then began to believe in the power of prayer. She had witnessed enough to know the miraculous effect it could have. But now, her prayers were for her — not the children, not other family members, not friends. In silence she could cry to Him. No matter that others misunderstood her, she had Him and His listening ear.

I am sure Mom was unaware that I was watching all this. I am sure she felt I was just as impatient and as much in a hurry to live my life and get on with things as anyone, when I would seemingly brush her off. But I was aware of her struggle, and I did see her study, and I did catch her tears and prayers.

When she couldn't find a place to be alone in the house, she might be found outside. I found her one night crying and praying out loud in the garden in back of the house. I was fifteen at the time and was unaware of her specific concerns. It might have been during some trying financial times, and while one of my brothers was away in the military. She hadn't heard me come up behind her, and I was too embarrassed to intrude. But I was also curious to know what was troubling her and had an impulse to help her if I could. Listening to her anguished pleadings touched and softened my heart. I learned a lesson that night about gardens and prayers I have never forgotten.

I felt, in that moment, that Mom was being attended to by someone who had prayed in another garden long ago, and had shed tears in supplication to the *only* One who could hear Him at the time. I had an epiphany—a revelation about how small we are in the big scheme of things but how significant the details of our lives are to One mightier than us all. Hard to describe, the impact was more powerful to me at that time than any string of words I might use trying to express it.

Without her knowing it, Mom had served me once more that night in my fifteenth year. I would later find my own gardens, my own places to go, and because of her example and what I had felt that dark and moonless Southern California evening, I knew I would never have to be alone.

Mom's courage in facing the silence and finding

another voice willing to listen to her reminds me to quiet my own life and listen more intently.

Holy scriptures describe that voice as a "still, small voice," a voice unlike any a noisy world might offer, a voice that takes a special awareness to hear. It is a soft voice that offers solutions, guidance, comfort, and peace. It is not heard with the natural ear but is discerned through contemplation, meditation, and prayer. It is a voice my mother has learned to hear.

Which makes me wonder: when the operation she had hoped would cure her failed, and Mom descended into a world of silence, was she dealt a "bad hand," or given a proverbial "bitter pill" to swallow?

Yes, by all accounts of those who do not know "the rest of the story," as Paul Harvey likes to say in his radio monologue. Viewed from one perspective, some would say Mom was given a "raw deal." The doctor let her down and messed up her life.

Fast forward from 1967 to 1988—twenty-one years after Mom's unsuccessful surgery. She and Dad were nearing seventy years of age and returning home after spending a year doing volunteer service for their church in another part of the country. Mom had long since adjusted to not being able to hear, but at that time, the chronic ringing in her ears had intensified. By then they were living in Idaho but were passing through Southern California, where they had lived while raising their family. She told Dad she would like to stop in and see our old family physician in Simi, California. Doctor Keith Baker was well aware of her condition, but there was no hope he could offer any relief. Mom's loss of hearing was the result of botched surgery, and there was nothing to suggest anything could be done after all those years.

Listening in the friendly manner he is famous for, Doctor Baker did the ear exam he had done so many times before. Not the surgeon who had performed the 1968 work, he nonetheless knew Mom's ailment and so started the procedures she was so accustomed to.

"It really rings," Mom told him. "It is so loud, so much louder than I have ever noticed over the last twenty years."

"You say it rings all the time?" *Shouldn't,* he thought to himself. *Even poorly done, the operation shouldn't produce such an effect.* Something told him to continue the examination, and then he had it!

Shocked, he worked and finally pulled from Mom's inner ear some surgical packing the original surgeon had carelessly left in there.

"Virginia! I am so, so sorry! I want to apologize for my profession. This is an absolute injustice to you. I know how much you have suffered!"

Mom and Dad looked with amazement at the cause of her deafness. What a discovery! An egregious mistake had been made by a careless physician. There were ample grounds for a massive malpractice suit.

But it was just like Mom and Dad to leave that in the past. Nothing was to be gained by seeking compensation now. In a strange way, it was a relief just to know what had caused the two decades of suffering. They would leave the anger where it lay—buried and forgotten.

Mom says the discovery felt as though something heavy had been lifted off her. She was relieved, not angry, as many might have been. She was also excited, grasping at a vain hope that she might be able to hear again. That was not to be. From all they could tell, Mom's surgery would have been a success back in 1968, but over twenty years, the surgical packing that had been left inside her inner ear had caused too much damage. With the packing removed the ringing diminished, and that seemed a blessing enough.

Though it doesn't help, Mom still wears a hearing aid. No one but she really knows why. Maybe it's because she is a woman of hope, someone who never gives up. Maybe she feels that taking it out would be a final surrender of sorts. Yes, she hears tones. But real vibrant and clear sounds that have meaning like the rest of us? No. That is something she will never enjoy again.

In a clumsy attempt to comfort her, I remind her that there is an awful lot of "sound and fury, signifying nothing" in the world—useless clanging, banging, crashing, noisy sounds, just as well left unheard. And I remind her that a lot of conversations are not uplifting and there is often too much useless banter in our world. But it is sad that she is not able to hear a great-grandbaby's first attempts to speak, terms of endearment whispered by loving family members and friends, and the notes of inspiring and beautiful music. Yet there is a music in her soul, and indeed in all souls at peace, and it plays unlike anything the rest of us might understand—unless of course we are in tune with the *inner ear*.

The other day I was troubled. Nothing new, just fatherly concerns, things Mom had observed me dealing with before. She often reminds me she prays for me. She did so again as I sat in her home that day, just before I departed for my four-hour drive home to Utah. I explained to Mom my fears for my adult son, now living temporarily with her, and some choices I wish he would make that could save him considerable grief.

My anxiety and concern stayed with me for those many miles. They were on my mind still as I arrived home and opened my e-mail. The only one received was from Mom. "Are you home?" she asked.

I knew she would worry. She fears, as mothers do, for the travels of her children, no matter their ages.

I quickly answered that I was safe and home. She could relax now. But that was not what was entirely on her mind. Another e-mail came back. It read in part:

"I am glad I am able to help some. My ears are

my big problem, but my mind still works well and is constantly going. . . . I am sorry about your miserable day with your son, and while he does things without thinking, he wants to do what's right and knows you love him. We talked about that. He seems to listen to me. Don't make yourself sick. . . . He'll come out of it. *Son, be still and be at peace.* I love you lots. Mom."

That comforting assurance made me think that she not only understands but is in tune with a higher source who is also aware of my anxiety as a parent. I took her advice to heart. I am being still, and I am listening with the inner ear as I pray for my child as Mom has prayed for me.

The day will come when she will hear music, and God will compensate her for the loss of hearing. But perhaps He already has. She understands and hears things most of the world cannot. She has taught me by example to listen carefully to the inner ear and the still, small voice that speaks to it.

Mom, thanks for teaching me to listen to the inner ear. I understand where to look for peace and can hear a voice that tells me I will never be alone.

CHAPTER 9

Kissing Santa Claus

*"You must remember this, a kiss is
still a kiss, a sigh is just a sigh. The fundamental
things apply, as time goes by."*
—*"As Time Goes By,"* Herman Hupfeld

Unlike some married couples, my parents were
never self-conscious about showing their
affection for one another. As children, we often
observed them kissing and hugging each other. It
was as much a part of the routine of our home as it
was for us to sit down together each evening for
dinner. And they lavished that same affection on
their children. As babies, toddlers, and little children, we were cooed over, cuddled, hugged, and

kissed by our parents. We grew up knowing we were adored. It was just the norm, a family thing.

"How ya doin', chicken?" was one of Dad's daily reminders to Mom that she held a special place in his heart. That was the question he always asked as he arrived home from work. It was an invitation for her to participate in their private little ritual, where they took time out from the family and where Mom was allowed to just be herself and vent if she needed to about the day, knowing he was listening. Openly loving Mom was one of the finest things Dad ever did for his children. We knew by the affectionate way he treated her that he loved our mother, and he provided us a great example to follow in our own marriages.

Mom reciprocated Dad's affection, and that was the basis of their lifelong love affair. In her unabashed acceptance of Dad's affection, Mom showed what a healthy love for a man could be like, and to that end she taught her boys and girls, without conscious effort, what a woman desires to be for her husband.

I admit that I may not have always followed my parents' example, but that doesn't mean the model they provided wasn't a good one or that it is out-moded or has been replaced by something better. Unrequited love may provide the best fodder for melancholy Country Western songs, but *requited* love is the best kind. And that is what my parents practiced openly, day in and day out.

But there comes a day, usually in your early teens, when some otherwise ordinary things begin to make you uncomfortable. Entering the curious and awkward phase of sexual awareness, it occurs to you that old people should not be doing certain things, like kissing and cuddling — at least not all the time.

I have a vivid memory of something I saw when I was eleven or twelve years old. It was Christmas Eve, and I got out of bed to sneak a peek into the living room, hoping to catch an early look at what Santa had left under the tree. What I saw was shocking. There was Dad, helping Mom place the gifts under and around the tree and tugging on her until she finally gave in. She kissed him!

Yes, indeed. Santa was Mom's great love, and the old guy acted like he was enjoying it! They kissed and giggled. It was disgusting. I couldn't bear to watch them behaving like that, so I snuck back to my room where I decided that it had to be the magic of the mistletoe. Had to be! No way two old people could act like teenagers. Hugging. Kissing. Giggling. It nearly made me ill.

I decided to let it go and went on with my life. They never let up, though. I just acted like I didn't notice during my teen years.

Don't get me wrong. They were always circumspect in their expressions of affection. Dad never treated Mom with anything but great respect and was never out of line. It was just that . . . well, hey, she was my *mother!*

I eventually got over being embarrassed by our parents' open expressions of affection and came to appreciate it for what it was—the unspoken symbol of their love for and loyalty to each other. They simply adored one another.

I just assumed that would automatically happen in my marriage but have learned, along with all six of my brothers, that working at it is a constant necessity. We took it for granted that it would come easy because Mom and Dad made it look that way.

I suppose they might have clued us in. Might

have informed us in some birds-and-bees talk how
the loving in a marriage works and how adoration
of your mate can last a lifetime, but they didn't.
They just showed us how it works, and I guess we
were expected to take note and learn.

Young love doesn't always blossom into a lifetime of devotion and loyalty, as the romantic
notions would suggest. But when it does, it is a
beautiful thing to see. That is what we were blessed
to observe in our parents' relationship. And one of
the finest things Mom did for her children was to
demonstrate, in so many unspoken ways, how
much she *adored* our dad.

When our family's Santa, the man who always
gave the best he had, was moments from death, I
saw yet another demonstration of Mom's devotion
to him. That tender scene has inspired me to want
to be a better man and has shaped my view of what
a man and a woman can ideally mean to each other.
It is fixed in my mind now and is just as poignant
to me as it was when it happened.

It was an April afternoon in 1994, and Dad had
been desperately ill and was struggling to breathe.
It was clear he couldn't survive much longer.

Mom was at his side, gently stroking the thin wisps of hair on his head. I was there also, holding his hand and giving silent gratitude for this man we loved. Playing in the background was a recording of Dad's favorite American choir, softly singing one of his favorite hymns—something we hoped would comfort and calm him in these final moments.

"You can go now, Grant. You can go, darling. Oh, darling, I love you so much," Mom said as she kissed his tired brow.

This was the concluding movement, the high point of a sonata of love, played out by these two over the more than fifty years they had loved each other. And in spite of the sacredness of the moment, it was being played out in crescendo, not diminuendo.

Dad opened his eyes one final time and turned his head toward me. Knowing perhaps that Mom couldn't hear him, he looked into my eyes intently and said the three most powerful and loving words one can express to another. I didn't interrupt Mom with my excitement at hearing him speak, the only words to leave his lips in days. I knew she needed to continue her goodbye.

"Goodbye, darling. You can go now," she repeated. "Oh, how I have loved you," she reminded him, and he sighed his final breath and was gone.

You already know that Mom is deaf. Dad couldn't have said anything she would have heard, but it didn't matter.

Kiss him in your dreams, dear Mother, and teach us how to love a man and, as men, be loved.

Your children are all older now. In the scheme of time, as fast as it goes by, we have a brief moment now to wait to see the jolly man, the happy face, the lovely man who adored you as much as you adored him.

He had loved her all he could in fifty years of togetherness and she knew it. It was her turn to be strong, bid farewell once again, as she had done when he went away to war so many years before. He will come back someday . . . Santa always does.

Thanks, Mom, for returning Santa's kiss and so openly loving Dad. It was one of the best gifts you ever gave us!

CHAPTER 10

"Just One Day at a Time"

"Most mothers are instinctive philosophers."
— HARRIET BEECHER STOWE

Mom is a contented lady and at peace. She has never walked an easy road or lived in luxury. Even now she lives simply, far from the comforts and ease of retirement communities, resorts, city life. But she continues to see blessings in what we might consider little things, and is alert to what really matters most.

I recorded it when she said, "A perfect life to me is just doing tasks well, one day at a time." I am sure she hadn't given great thought to her words being shared with the world in a book, but just simply with a son. She understands the way to obtain contentment, which is: *Know how to be satisfied with what you have and make the best of it.*

"You have to just live one day at a time, Son," has been a faithful and true statement she has used hundreds of times during conversations about events, life's challenges, and the surprises that never seem to end.

Dad used to remind me, "Son, don't worry about things you can't do anything about, and don't worry about things you can." Some of the greatest advice ever given has been simple and yet startling at the same time. Maybe that's because most of the answers to life's great quests begins with "Just one day at a time."

Mom and Dad made these two overlapping philosophies work for them and tried to instill the same virtues in us, their nine children.

Dad definitely handled stress and worry differently than Mom. When I asked him how he was able to take things so calmly, he explained, "After the German artillery shelling I went through on that beach at Anzio during World War II, nothing much gets to me." He'd stared death in the face through one hundred and twenty days of constant bombardment and survived. During much of that time, there was little he could do to prevent one of those enemy shells from landing on him, and he had decided that worrying about it was not a productive use of time. The only day that mattered was the one he was living—that was the only day he needed to worry about. That does not mean Dad didn't have concerns. He just had serenity and poise about trials. That was a blessing to Mom.

Mom, while admittedly not always unruffled about life's vagaries, the financial and other stresses, maintained a strong and inherent belief that God knew what was happening and cared, and that the best way to handle problems is "one day at a time."

So she did. And I watched. I watched her do all she could on any given day and then in the evening embrace our father and "let it go."

"Worry and stress will kill you," Dad would tell me. "Do all you can today and then let the Lord do the rest," Mom would tell me.

A traditional and religious woman of great faith, Mom has always loved the Proverbs of King

Solomon from the Old Testament. I think her favorite passage has been chapter 3, verses 5 and 6:

Trust in the Lord with all thine heart; and lean not unto thine own understanding. In all thy ways acknowledge him, and he shall direct thy paths.

So now I can look back five decades and test the wisdom of a mother's love and sayings. God did something extremely good, right, and worth more than all the wealth He might pour down when He gave men mothers! She taught me:

Life is lived one day at a time.
Love is built just one day at a time.
Relationships are built one day at a time.
Memories are forever.

One day at a time, Mom had waited for her soldier to come home from World War II. That meant not knowing until long after a battle was over whether or not Grant Pratt had survived it. That meant living in daily fear of receiving one of those dreaded telegrams that began: "The Department of the Army regrets to inform you . . ."

One day at a time, she had endured the torment of wondering how her two firstborn sons were doing in Vietnam from 1965 to 1967. When sons and daughters were far from home for years at a time, she endured the worry, one day at a time.

One day at a time—through ups, downs, financial reversals, feeding, clothing, caring for, educating, and counseling nine children—she lived her life.

One day at a time she built a strong family with Dad, beginning in 1945 with her marriage and continuing in her current role as a grandmother and great-grandmother, giving love and dispensing advice in 2004.

We live just one day at a time.

Now I know why Dad loved her so much and why the wisest king to live among men ended his Proverbs with this thought about virtuous women. His lines, written thousands of years ago, read as if he knew my mother, and knew what we, her children, think of her:

> *Who can find a virtuous woman? for her price is far above rubies.*
>
> *The heart of her husband doth safely trust in her, so that he shall have no need of spoil.*
>
> *She will do him good and not evil all the days of her life.*

She seeketh wool, and flax, and worketh willingly with her hands.

She is like the merchants' ships; she bringeth her food from afar. . . .

She layeth her hands to the spindle, and her hands hold the distaff.

She stretcheth out her hand to the poor; yea, she reacheth forth her hands to the needy. . . .

Her husband is known in the gates, when he sitteth among the elders of the land. . . .

Strength and honor are her clothing; and she shall rejoice in time to come.

She openeth her mouth with wisdom; and in her tongue is the law of kindness.

She looketh well to the ways of her household, and eateth not the bread of idleness.

Her children arise up, and call her blessed; her husband also, and he praiseth her.

Many daughters have done virtuously, but thou excellest them all. . . .

Give her of the fruit of her hands; and let her own works praise her in the gates.

(KJV Proverbs 31:10–14, 19–20, 23, 25–29, 31)

Mom is in her eighties and what younger people sometimes refer to as "an old person." Up until recently she would look me in the eye and ask, "Jim, do I look like an old lady to you?"

See, the older I get, the more I understand what really "old" people are thinking. I'm reminded of the handsome actor Cary Grant and what his mother is reported to have said after calling him on the telephone to chastise him on the way he looked. After a particularly outstanding televised perform-ance, but one in which his hair had begun to gray, she let him know it bothered her. The generous and affable actor insisted to his mother that he didn't mind his hair turning gray.

"But it makes me seem so old," his aged mother lashed back.

What would you say if your mother were to ask you if she is an "old lady"? Well, if you are like me you will try for as much silence mixed with diplo-macy as possible. My answer has always been, "Your children are all over fifty or nearly so. What do you think?"

"Well, I guess that makes me old," she'll say.

I say nothing. Just smile, nod my head slightly,

and let her know it's really, "Just one day at a time, Mom."

She wants things to be finished. Have things in order. Her children and posterity to be "squared away." She is a mother, and doesn't like to leave things undone. She is lonely though—for her partner, the worry-free man who kissed her under the Christmas tree those many years ago.

One day at a time, Mom—It means waiting to kiss her husband and once again be with him and other loved ones on God's schedule and not on her own.

Thanks, Mom, for showing the way. Now I know a perfect life is built by doing our tasks well, one day at a time.

CHAPTER 11

"Just Close Your Eyes"

*"And wherever we may turn, this lesson we shall learn,
a boy's best friend is his mother."*
—JOSEPH P. SKELLEY

"Dear Mom and Dad,

"Everything is fine here in Vietnam. I'm with a lot of good people and we are well protected. Everyone carries a gun, so don't worry. The people are grateful to have us here. A little bit dangerous at times, but I'll be okay. The food is different, but there is plenty of it. Well, just to let you know I'm here and well.

"Mom, whenever I need you I just close my eyes! Love . . ."

Ever wonder why letters to parents are almost

always addressed to Moms first? Ever wonder why boys never really tell their Moms the truth about the harsh conditions they sometimes face when they leave home?

I recall the letters from my two older brothers who served in Vietnam at the war's peak buildup, and the anxiety my mother and father experienced when a letter did not arrive every couple of weeks. I recall writing my own weekly letters from far off South America in my early twenties. Most of the letter's contents were truthful, but all the stuff about "things are fine" . . . those were almost entirely lies. I have prayed for death only three times in my life. All three times were during separate incidents when I had fallen nearly mortally ill in the country of Peru. Mom never knew about that, though. See, no man will knowingly let his mother suffer; no, not ever, if he can avoid it.

A mother is special to the man she rears, and her name is always first on his lips when he describes home cooking and last on his lips when he is sick or near death.

My heart was touched as I recently watched the war in Iraq unfolding. It was April 2003, and U. S.

troops had just entered Baghdad. Television crews accompanied them. One of the first images transmitted from the war zone back to the United States was a handwritten message scrawled by a Marine on the wall of a bullet scarred building:

"Hi Mom. I'm okay. Will be home soon." Then the word "Love . . ." followed by the initials of the young Marine. No mention of Dad, but not out of disrespect. The Marine just knew, as men instinctively do, that Dad understands.

What happens when the television camera singles out on the bench the football player who has just scored the winning touchdown?

As his teammates slap him on the back and he struggles to balance his cup of Gatorade, invariably he turns to the camera, flashes the victory sign, and mouths the words, "Hi, Mom!" And these are grown men!

We leave home for various reasons when we finish our high-school years. Some of us go off to get more schooling. Some leave home to give service to country, religion, or social organizations. To get a job or career started or just to "see the world" are all reasons why a boy or girl leaves Mom, security, comforts, and the familiar aroma of her cooking behind.

Strange, isn't it, how Mom seems to be ever present after we leave her home? We see her in hundreds of little things daily. Her voice seems to come into our minds. Mild or scolding, it warms us and gives us courage to face the day, just as it has so many times before.

In life and in death, the word *mother* has been uttered in every earthly language to venerate the woman who gave life, believed in, and sustained the man passing through his mortal tests. And equally sacred to the child-adult away from her touch is the meaning in the word *home*. *Home* and *Mother*. They are almost synonymous.

Far too many of the tests young men will face in early manhood are found on battlefields. But no finer tribute can be paid a mother than by a son or daughter who, facing a test of life or death, calls upon memories of Mom for courage.

The words of an American soldier, written to his mother from the battlefields of Iraq, moved me to tears. His body had just been recovered and among his personal items was found a final letter home, written in the fear he might not make it back. These words could have been spoken by any soldier on any battlefield from any time in the history of warfare. His sentiments echo all those of the men who breathed their last breath in combat. PFC Diego Fernando Rincon of Conyers, Georgia, wrote: *"Mother will be the last word I'll say. Your face will be the last picture that goes through my eyes."*

A suicide bomber killed Rincon and three other soldiers at a checkpoint near Rajaf on March 29, 2003, as they defended freedom on that foreign soil.

But soldiers of every race, and young men and women growing up and finally growing old, never forget the tender woman and the sacred title that describes her: Mom, Mamá, Mère, Madre, Mütter, and a thousand more.

Mom . . . we say goodbye to you when we grow up, but you never leave us alone. Your face, your voice, your love echoes throughout our lives, calling us back to simpler days and times. Now and then we come home in our mind's eye. You are there waiting with good food and a warm heart. We are listening to you, feeling your tender embrace, the kiss on the cheek, and our hearts are gladdened.

Mom, I'm closing my eyes now.

Whenever we need you, no matter where we are, all we have to do is close our eyes, smile, and walk through that door calling out: "Mom! I'm home . . ."

CHAPTER 12

FIRST, LAST, AND ALWAYS

*"Darling Mama, I had always prayed to show
my love by doing something famous for you. . . . Nothing
you ever did to me was anything but loving. I have
no memories but love and devotion."*

—GENERAL GEORGE S. PATTON JR.

I will never forget Mom's guiding love when she
reminded me as a young man to warm myself
with her oatmeal, nor the taxi rides she gave me
when I was strong enough to walk where I needed
to go.

I can't forget the cheerleader Virginia Pratt was
on winning nights and losing nights when she came
with my worn and tired construction worker father
to my high school football games, nor will I ever

forget her gentle mending of a physical body scraped or cut or beat up from playing too hard.

Although I knew better then and now, somehow Mom always made me feel as if I were the *only* son. She owned a magic potion, an elixir that never emptied from a bottle she must have kept hidden somewhere.

I know the 1965 song "Love Potion Number Nine" was titled by a lyricist who must have observed Mom in action with us seven boys and two girls.

I was born in struggle. Pronounced clinically dead, I had been given up, but Mom told me that while on the delivery table, she had prayed to God to let me live. I wonder if, over the years, she hadn't sometimes regretted that because of the heartache I sometimes brought her. But know this, that a mother's prayer from the day this child was born has been worth more than all the honors and wealth the world could ever bestow.

Moms sacrifice. They give it all. In giving life they are often called upon to give their own. Can there be a greater love?

No, for it must be that there was a law decreed

in the heavens there would always be one person a boy or girl could count on. Notwithstanding the greatness of fathers and all they do, mothers are first, last, and always in the hearts of their children.

First, last, always . . . Mom, you are and always will be number one in the heart of this son and your other sons and daughters. God bless you now and forever.

Mom, The Woman who Made Oatmeal Stick to My Ribs is a companion volume to *Dad: The Man Who Lied to Save the Planet,* published regionally in 2003 by Shadow Mountain and nationally in 2004.

The following, "How Ya Doin', Chicken?" is chapter 3 from that earlier book.

CHAPTER 3

"How Ya Doin', Chicken?"

O ne of my fondest memories of my parents' relationship was my father's practice of speaking tender and loving words to my mother.

In the brief birds and bees talk he gave me as I headed into marriage, Dad told me, "I'd rather be a gentleman and receive your mother's love because she wants to give it, than force mine upon her." That really struck me. See, Dad was a *gentle* man by nature, and now I don't think he ever consciously planned or plotted ways to win his wife's affection. He just seemed to always do the right thing by Mom.

When young people marry, they usually have un-realistic expectations about what their relationship will be. Those expectations are spawned in the courtship where each partner is on his or her best behavior. Unless the courtship is lengthy, it's possible that the two starry-eyed people will have seen only the best side of each other prior to the marriage ceremony.

Being newly "in love" prompts a man or a woman to be considerate and thoughtful in an attempt to impress the object of his or her affection. During courtship, gifts are given, courtesy practiced, and tokens of affection frequently exchanged.

Blinded somewhat by excitement and romance, the woman assumes that her man will always be the considerate, gentle, and loving prince she has found. The man is sure that his princess will forever be the sweet, smiling, thoughtful person he discovered while dating. She enters marriage convinced she couldn't have found a more perfect man; he is certain his bride is the most precious thing who ever lived. The embodiment of perfection, each assumes that after they are married, sparks will fly every time they look at each other.

What happens to those sparks after a few years? Where does the perfect man and woman go? Men sometimes complain that their spouse's concern for the children's needs, her professional work, or other interests take precedence over him. She frequently feels that his job, his hobbies and friends, and the pressures of meeting other obligations diminish her importance to him. Often lost in the drudgery of daily routines, there seems to be no room for the romance that originally brought them together, and each mourns the loss of the frequent intimacy of those early married years.

I have had the honor of being entrusted with the precious correspondence my mother and father exchanged while he was away during World War II. In those letters I found a genuinely romantic man and woman, who freely communicated their love, longing, friendship, and fidelity.

There exists in my parents' war-time letters to each other a constant, unabashed expression of adoration between sweethearts. They unselfconsciously addressed each other as "Darling," without any premonition of how terribly sappy it might sound to their children or grandchildren fifty years later. If such expressions are sappy, maudlin, or schmaltzy, as some cynics suggest, then lovers of that era were at the very least a bunch of happy saps.

There is also something honest in those letters that I find enormously appealing. To communicate in those days meant hand writing a letter and believing the postman could deliver it before a month went by or before the soldier died in battle. Written in longhand, great feeling was poured into every carefully chosen word. In our day of easy telephone communication or instant email exchanges, we perhaps can't imagine the thrill it must have been to receive such a letter or the excitement with which lovers in my parents' generation pored over the words, savoring each expression of affection, longing for the reunion that seemed so far off and uncertain.

You may think I am romanticizing all of this—that a chaste love affair such as I have described my parents having is idealized or improbable. I don't believe so. See, they had something largely lost to us now; shining armor still existed. There is a certain appealing flavor to the mutual adoration found in their letters and in speech; an unhurried and tender part of courtship was the manner in which they communicated from the heart — the knight to his lady, the lady to her knight.

Watch any romantic movie made in the 1930s, '40s, or '50s. The screenwriters turned out wonderful love stories, without explicitly depicting sex. Limited by industry codes and the mores and standards of the time, filmmakers found a way to create love scenes that left much to the imagination and in many ways generated more passion than today's blatant and gratuitous dramatizations. Filmmakers then could never have imagined doing what their counterparts of today are permitted to do. To audiences of my parents' generation, it would have not been real, and in fact moviegoers would have been embarrassed by the vulgarity of it all.

That is not to say my parents' generation were all saints, were all perfect, or that there wasn't such a thing as sexual promiscuity in those days. It obviously has always existed, but it was not generally condoned or glamorized, and when it was portrayed in the movies, it wasn't graphically shown. There was still such a thing as the depiction of guilt and resulting consequences for choices. That was a reflection of the mores and standards most Americans embraced. They were, and those still with us are, to their credit, great romantics.

Why I find the brand of love and romance of my parents' era so appealing might be more easily understood if I share, as Paul Harvey says in his daily radio monologue, "the rest of the story."

Having found each other, my parents had to endure two and a half years of wartime separation before they could marry. They kept their romance alive through written correspondence, which only increased their desire for each other. Dad revealed to me that he was as excited as any man to experience the intimacies of marriage but that he and Mom had waited until after they were married. Contrary to the way things are often done these days, they exercised restraint and patience in order to do it right, according to the expectations of their day.

That kind of morality was not uncommon in those times, and it helped lay the foundation for enduring marriages.

As I reflect on my parents' relationship and recall Dad's considerate treatment of Mom, I realize that his conduct was deeply rooted in the culture of those times. He was conditioned to be patient and gentlemanly, she to be demure and chaste.

Contrast that with our current situation. We live in a world where instant gratification is the thing and where we demand *drive-through* convenience, *fast-food* service, and *express* check-out lanes. Computers enable us to retrieve data instantly, expedite our purchases, and communicate in the flickering of an eye. Most of us are unwilling to wait for *anything.*

We live at a pace that my folks and their friends could never have imagined. They grew up and lived in a time where most bread was still hand-kneaded at home, television was yet unborn, radio was limited to a couple of stations, cars rarely traveled over fifty miles per hour, music was Crosby and Sinatra crooning, and Mabel at the phone company still connected you at reverse warp speed. The "EAT GAS FOOD" signs along America's highways, encouraging you to stop your car, only signaled the beginning of the modern age where you could do more than one thing in one place.

It was against that backdrop that Dad wooed

Mom and in which he tapped into the secret that kept their love alive. Dad wasn't book-trained or college-bred, but he intuitively knew the everyday things he could do to make Mom happy.

After I had married, I once turned to Dad for some advice. Some of the magic my wife and I had discovered in each other while dating had diminished, and I wondered how I could rekindle some of that. As muddle-brained as any man, I was missing the great secret.

I don't think my father stopped and thought: "Now I am going to hit that son of mine right between the eyes with a profound statement on the subject of loving a woman, one he will never forget."

What he said was this: "Son, your mother knows I love her because no matter what each day brings, I try to tell her so and show that I do by listening. Just treat her like you did back when you thought she was perfect." Then he taught me the great truth:

"Son, just adore her, and everything will be fine."

He somehow understood that after dating, after

courtship, and after marriage, a woman still desires to be *adored*.

The wisdom was just good old-fashioned philosophy from his day, and it still works.

I'd gotten terribly busy with life. My wife had, too. We were on a frenzied pace to save the world, our local church, the kids' soccer team, the PTA, and the elementary school from disaster but had forgotten about this *adoration* thing. See, to adore someone takes time and effort, the same kind of time and effort we had invested during our dating years. Dad was reminding me of something I had forgotten.

Adoring the girl he married was the finest thing Dad ever did for Mom, and it was one of the finest things he did for us seven boys. It is a lesson I am understanding with clarity only now.

Webster's defines *adore* as: "1. To worship as divine 2. To love or honor greatly; idolize 3. To like very much." To be adored is more than receiving flowers or gifts, although those certainly are ways to remember the person you love.

Often, after the five of us boys under sixteen years old had pushed our mom to the brink of tears, after we had her wagon surrounded and she felt she was just about to take the last arrow, my father would walk in from work. Tired and dirty from a hard day's labor in construction, he would look at my frazzled mother, take her in his arms, and say, "How ya doin', chicken?"

Never mind that he carried the odor of manual labor, dust and sweat still clinging to him, she was willing to be held. There was an embrace, eye contact that invited her to ventilate her frustration, and a confirmation of her worth. Dad not only physically shielded her from our antics but also met her emotional needs. That, I have come to know, was a major part of their intimacy.

Dad probably couldn't have articulated it, but he intuitively practiced what Henry Ward Beecher, nineteenth century author and preacher, taught: "Do not keep the alabaster boxes of your loves and tenderness sealed up until your friends are dead. Fill their lives with sweetness. Speak approving, cheering words while their ears can hear them and while their hearts can be thrilled by them."

I doubt there exists more precious words in any language than the simple three, "I love you." I certainly cannot hear them enough. Spoken by my wife, my daughter, my son, my brothers, sisters, and friends—those three words give meaning to life and are always thrilling to hear.

"How ya doin', chicken?" might not sound like "I love you," or "Darling, I adore you," but Mom knew. It was their little code.

What Dad taught me when I was struggling in the early years of my marriage to understand the secrets of a good one—one as strong as he and Mom had achieved—was this:

Son, just adore her, and everything will be fine.